A·FIRST·BOOK·OF
DO'S AND DON'TS

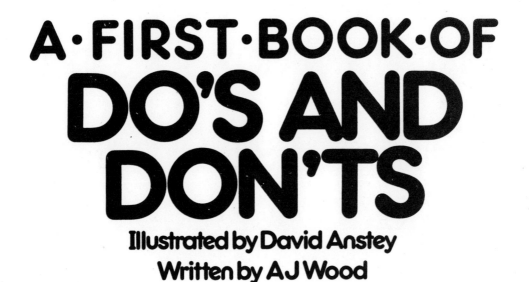

A·FIRST·BOOK·OF
DO'S AND DON'TS

Illustrated by David Anstey

Written by A J Wood

MODERN PUBLISHING
A Division of Unisystems, Inc.
New York, New York 10022

What do dinosaurs do?

Dinosaurs DO eat
their breakfast...

Dinosaurs DON'T
spill crumbs on the floor.

Dinosaurs DO
keep their
bedrooms neat...

Dinosaurs DON'T leave their toys all over the floor.

Dinosaurs DO
tie their shoelaces
and button their coats...

Dinosaurs DON'T jump in puddles on the way to school.

Dinosaurs DO brush their teeth...

Dinosaurs DON'T eat too many sweets.

Dinosaurs DO
go to bed
when they are told...

Dinosaurs DON'T
stay up late watching TV...

At least, not very often.

The End